Void Studies

RACHAEL BOAST was born in Suffolk in 1975.
Sidereal (Picador, 2011) won the Forward Prize for
Best First Collection and the Seamus Heaney Centre
for Poetry Prize. She is editor of *The Echoing Gallery:
Bristol Poets and Art in the City* (Redcliffe Press).
Pilgrim's Flower (Picador, 2013) was shortlisted
for the Griffin Prize. She lives in Bristol.

Rachael Boast

Void Studies

PICADOR

First published 2016 by Picador
an imprint of Pan Macmillan
20 New Wharf Road, London N1 9RR
Associated companies throughout the world
www.panmacmillan.com

ISBN 978-1-5098-1145-8

1 3 5 7 9 8 6 4 2

A CIP catalogue record for this book is available from the British Library.

Printed and bound by CPI Group (UK) Ltd, Croydon, CR0 4YY

Visit **www.picador.com** to read more about all our books
and to buy them. You will also find features, author interviews and
news of any author events, and you can sign up for e-newsletters
so that you're always first to hear about our new releases.

Contents

I

II

POEMS OF THE LOST POEM

Void Studies

I

Afterlife

Late nights like unopened letters
the fold coming unstuck

from this one in the moist air
the message made prescient

by the way in which a wave
lifting from the surface of itself

could be lifted further
enough to reach into it and grasp

from under its erratic stars
the unwritten hour before dawn

A Second Time

Time stops where the vision
left off and the miracles began

the freak fall of snow
storm that opened the inner door

then the front and back until
the walls turned deep red

home was not where home was
the hallway an impossible wind tunnel

for the swarm you left behind
the portal by chance still open

Reverdie

Climbing over the gate into a garden
for residents only or so it says

being the perfect place to notice
a green thought gaining ground

from underneath the dreams
I bring with me which seem to have

more reality than can be accounted for
I hold the key to this privacy

to pursue once again the magical study
of the happiness nothing escapes

Sunday

The smell of sunlight on river-water
in shocks and tints ruins the calm mirror

of sleep and the disciplines of the dark.
The pushy oars of rowers dissemble and mark

the surface leaving a trail of peacock eyes
in their wake while half-asleep in the ultraviolet

I almost believe in the sky's huge blue terrace
trembling. I've seen you shield yourself from this

fabulous Chaos the day springs on us,
dreaming yourself awake in fits and starts.

Night Vision

Back you go to the late hour's work
of the sound of the night

against where you live your life
within a whereabouts unknown.

But now her dance like no other
includes you, knew you all along

for how you keep time, the elegance
of the way you move slowly at first

across the room, then gathering the dark,
then brave in the doorway of her arms.

Rooms of the World

At the ancient inn
by the side of the road

where it's said
the rolling hills speak

of labyrinths unlocking
interiors of detail

these five keys behind glass
each giving a password

for another world
turn by themselves

Anonymous

For the sake of the old ways
I lean over the footbridge

and compose in my mouth
a lyric of saliva for the water

seeing my face fragment
then disappear recollecting

itself again as the bridle path
becomes the spine

of a well-thumbed volume
written by no one

Snow

As though it had waited all year in the wings
of a sleep-eyed white angel to fall

and did so in an hour, assured of its own
answerless light cast across the garden,

while ice crystals melt from the bright lettering
upheld in the trees overnight,

everything is lost to the river's deep lay
and to the low note sustained in its shadows,

the roads give and take nothing,
and you can't get home, although you're home.

Airtime

Breaking my fast with earth and stones, or worse, eating
the masonry of old churches, the boulders of floods,

you reminded me of my new copy of *Études néantes*
I killed a fly with twenty-two years ago, how the nail

in the wooden beam entered through the back cover,
the index, the last poems, and pierced them.

Here I am, up in the air, leaving your studious island
where everything turns like a page – heads, phrases,

street corners, the statue of Galileo, moods of suspense
and elevation. And after the taste of violets, nothing.

Night Porter

Saint of the late hour whose step
is a sudden altar holding the door

for those whose book of whys
and wherefores is lost in a coat pocket

their movements measured by the stars
and not by the sun he unburdens the faces

of the afterhours emerging from parks
and tapas bars and relieves them

until in a second their derangement
which had become so critical evaporates

The Script of Sleep

The right words formed in my mind
backlit by the hum of their origin

yet even as they brightened into line
I fell asleep inside them

too tired to begin. If accident
has design, then here it is,

the gaps unfilled, no artifice.
Is the door into the oak hard to find?

No. It's where the scent of soft mud
mingles with the blood of the stones.

Quicksilver

The more I look the less there is of me
on a clear day by the edge of the water

in the moment when a memory surfaces
of the thoughts of another who at the time

said nothing but in a sudden movement
of their hand held the silence as if it were

a living thing: sleep-creature caught
in a wave transmitting – as now –

the same reflected light dreaming rapidly
along the length of a willow tree.

Seeing Double

Waning in the night house of Mercury
I return to her carrying a secret

the colour of a dawn sun above a horizon
of tree tops in a pointed sky strung

with the starlight of slow-moving time
clarified in the mirror where she rises

slipping from one bright hour to another
seeing double not from the corner of my eye

but from the middle looking again
as she couples her fortune of silver downriver

Human Torch

The night is off limits as you become
the view out of which I make

our shapes focus into one steady beam
lifted across the sleeping woods

shining out of the need not so much
for making sense of things as for the sense

made to originate from a requisite trance –
which is why I ask for a light, *this way*

this way, should you think to be out as late
as this, in this autumn of red paths.

Pleasant Thought for Morning

Hiding your face in my neck
and hiding your hands in my hair

hiding your lips on my lips
to stop the words before I speak

hiding in the space around
the space I have dressed you in

wings of hardened spirit.
Angelot, a new day is here,

hide your sobs and feed me
the slow pearls of dew drops.

Moment

Eyelids painted with eyes
the lips of cold fire

and the echo of snow
below the water

and deeper still
where into the bed

of the river we fell
in that stopped hour

we saw the moon grow full
a thousand times over

Secret Alphabets

After an hour it was clear there was nothing
to say we didn't both already know

that couldn't be said better in the act
of lifting a fork of fish eggs to my mouth

which is how we continued the exchange:
a piece of bread torn in two in return

for your sea bass, a sip of Cuvée Paradis
for my Château Néant, invisible fruit

softening on your tongue becoming
the unwritten notes of a dark song.

Testament

In my sleep the figure in a dream
chiselling at a rock face

in the Lomond Hills
reveals through the granite's

dark weather the golden lettering
which causes sweating.

As ever it is night without end
in a place that doesn't begin

yet he keeps rising to his task
caught up in the echo of his work.

The Call

Stepping through the last of the sky
held by half-asleep mirrors

of the rain storm along the path
by the river where over

the other side the trees uphold
a language picking away

the fabric of reality, the woods
rising with everything to say

at once, with black wings,
with sound shuffling the air.

Return of the Song

Notes on the tongue
with the right measure

of air at play between
the image of song

and of wine
in double staves

heard in our land
a contralto

becoming the key
to the door of the wind

Poem of the Dream

At some ungodly hour
the poet calls it a day

and drowns
the dawn's cockerel

once and for all
from his stronghold

of using words
to lengthen the night

keeping its seasons
tempered with excess of light

Night of Echoes

Remembering I hadn't finished Cocteau's
L'Ange Heurtebise while on the edge of sleep

and that the reason for this was down
to how the living word lifting off the page

migrates into wings of watered silk
with which we reach into our dreams

to carry on the fine conversation
we've been having about one thing or another

in translation I heard you approaching
the same threshold from the opposite direction

II

The Glass-hulled Boat

Waking at lunchtime to a subdued sky
bemused by how the pivots of sleep

came loose I thought I saw you at the back
of the Tower Belle only it would have been

you some time ago with your hair full of rain
and the sound of rain making for starboard

past the splayed passengers towards the bar
for another vodka and tonic or any other

see-through intoxicant while the slap of the wake
of a parallel life rises to the left and to the right

Double Exposure

Looking from the other side of the river
some hours later he recalls

he must have been on the balcony
in full view but still unknown

as if invisible, seen to sit out the hours
of the afternoon and not much else;

sees himself slightly altered from afar
while continuing to walk through

the laughter of autumn, only half believing
how quickly all this can change.

Album

The right decision was to push away
all vanity and all satisfaction,

going so far as to burn the furniture
and the beams from the ceiling

of his next-to-nothing garret
to keep the fire of the Great Work

alight, and, if need be, throwing
the entire room into it so that

what is left is nothing but the work,
thought latching onto thought and pulling.

Clair de lune

after Apollinaire

Mellifluent moon on the lips of the crazy
tonight the orchards and the towns are greedy

the stars are the affinities of the bees
of this luminous honey that drips from the vines

for all that is sweet falls from the sky
each ray of moonlight a ray of honey

so hidden I envisage a golden fortuity
I fear the sting of the fire of the Arcturian bee

who placed in my hands these delusory rays
and took its moon-honey to the rose of the winds

Wine Bar

As their eyes close into the brief moment
before two lips touch their irises

will lift out of view so that he's not
kissing her but kissing the deep

red room where behind the streetlight
behind the shutters can be heard

the bird that sings through the night
a song about how love cannot

entirely belong to us not because
it wants to but because it must.

The White Sun

The field deepens towards
a far line where the trees

and the village church
in the indifferent haze are one

and the same continuous
apparition of a veil. You realize

there is nothing to look forward to,
it being neither night nor day,

a white sun giving the sky
directions to nowhere.

Atrocious fanfare

Stopping for lunch of meat and wine
in the Maison Bleue on the off chance

you weren't there so the waitress took
your glass and by the next one

I was ascending to heaven
via the usual hellish path

to the sound of falling cutlery
while the undreamed-of work

transforms into a golden hurrah!
and with this I refill your missing glass

Dream of the Poem

This side of the night you're a blues singer
who sees everything that's going on

in the bar and, with soft eyes, notices
a stranger in the corner with his hands folded

over his hat. The name of the bar, Heaven,
and in the basement of Heaven, wine ageing

in oak barrels in the dark of the moon.
The stranger, who says he is asleep, dreams

of unpicked grapes growing full on the vine
that has wound itself around you.

Fireplace

Looking for the outline of a bird
in the ashes seeing only the edges

of worlds breaking off from the rapid
conversation of fire with nothing left

to compare them to in an unexpected
arousal detaching from the body's breath –

the self emptying of the self-emptying
raison d'être – distrusting where anything

might settle in a sudden rush of air
a flame opens its wings.

Heat Wave

Late nights like unsent letters
written straight off

on the trail not of thought
but of how the breezes

in the doorway become miracles
as I leave the kitchen table

moving from one room to another
waiting for the names of friends

and angels of the wound
the storm has forgotten

Flash of Lightning

Slowly unravelling
the silence

at the margin of things
the waking light

shows us the work
we've done already

seeing as what runs
down through the willow

is the rain that still falls
after the rainfall

Door of the Rose

No one would visit
the Fountain House,

not until spring changed
the way the light

deflected from the river
in silver blossom.

He held her like a rose
close to his chest –

night porter to its door
of glass petal.

Eleventh Hour

My hands of paper
an open book

five-leafed
making a pass

where the stairs take us
sliding along the scale

with lips of music
for the reach of a kiss

in the dark which is
a harmonica

For one night only

All in good time the night arrives
that makes the heart a phial

for the bee-sting you left in its chamber
as I focus on you from inside this

obscure mirror where you are all
it can contain without breaking.

The sky will pause for its lazuli hour
beyond the dark opening

at last in full swing the yellow
and black door of the morning.

Another hive

To say I'd push open the door
again to say I'd let you in

to what the swarm
was articulating

inside a transverse flute
inside a fire of keys

reaching that pitch
where I slip from your grasp of me

into air over and over
again I felt myself vanishing

Ten string serenade

You took the bread from my fingers,
glancing down for a moment

at my breasts like poppy fields.
Soon you'll move from one room

to another, listening for the music
you always fall asleep to, a late echo

of stars. I raise a glass to the night
your eyes stayed open on mine

as the storm and its honey-glow
lit up the drunk night of the soul.

You tried the door

The first drops of rain, a pulse in the leaves,
enough to make aspirin by rubbing

my fingers where my fingers shouldn't be,
something here remains of love

in the slow hours of imagined time
recovering in the afterlife as surprising

as what came before I searched on both sides
trying to locate myself where you are

a downpour and a flash of light
under the willow, under the night.

Reverie

Lasting for months
in a place which is both

portal and limbo,
night of echoes –

what have we become?
I remember nothing

of how we made it happen –
a woman walking out

of a painting
with an alabaster jar.

Shattered

A lake can only hold
so much rainwater

then overflows its mirror
breaking up into details

of the picture
impossible to gather again

the original image
we glimpsed now lost

in this drop of what is
cupped in your hands

The Other Woman

Applying wisdom to the flesh
was easier than expected –

already encrypted in the moons
of the fingernails, it was true,

your vision. Here it comes again:
the fine rain falling over fields

and trees could almost be a woman's face,
full of unhurried tenderness.

It seems you've known her a long time
yet never once has she stayed the night.

Contretemps

The last time I looked
it was still twelve o'clock

at the paper mill on the estuary
where the cries of seabirds

carry on for longer, fastening
their sound to the air.

It can't be avoided,
the half-empty carafe

of the only hour we have
always the hour

Château Néant

Door after door but with the same key
of cold iron unlocking them all

one to another leading on
to the room in the middle of nowhere

where you go to work the forge
of the dream of disrepair.

Stones sweat gold, copper and mercury.
A swarm of bees appears

from hammered metal
leaving an aftertaste of black honey.

Poems of the Lost Poem

From the French

I've given up remembering the words
of the poem written for you in a language
I had no hold over; letters of white light
on disappearing pages you might say
at heart were Sapphic in their largesse
and in the integrity of their brokenness —
and now even more so, well travelled
and in shreds; a double loss I can't help
but rhyme myself with, as if I could undo
who it is you've married yourself to
or said you had as you reached
to take a flower from the vase,
your voice lifting from the speaking earth
to the sky of few words, lost there . . .

Autumnal

A keen fear of words and the dark fruit
of words ripens in my hand, my body
overworked, negotiating pain, pushing
to find the vine on which the language grows.
I hide things in the mouth of the ground
for the ground to hoard them until
it is ready to speak, then offer a glass
to the increasing darkness, hoping
to fill it with a glint of myself.
The month will pass quickly, mothering
its oracles, gathering its blue robes
and shaking out the blue echoes
of servitude, and from the rich soil
of these difficulties I'll savour a brilliant wine.

Special Reserve

When you leave you never quite leave,
keeping me at the edge of your vision
as the days fill with other people
whose voices now and then rise
above the radio you seldom switch off
for how it drowns in sonatas
the events of a day and cleanses them,
even when asleep, or when, if ever,
you think back to what happened
before what happened before
and find me again, with not much to say,
sitting on the bank of the river with you
speaking in soft voices of the commonplace,
for the heart must surely speak that way.

Orpheus's Cloak

Night's blue prelude dripping white petals
at the edge of the garden leading
to the curve of the river's attention
as the rope slackens on this cold night,
stepping down onto the prow to get level
with the water, to look through its mirror
by waiting for that slow change of self
to otherness and breathe in its air
of abeyance. The moon is fully aware,
floating in a ballet of dark silver,
as the hour retains a surprising pleasure
no different from the sleep of flowers.
I need to delay my leave-taking,
be ever at the edge of these things.

Ranchera

She'll sing as if having downed
more than one glass of strong wine,
and loosening herself up gradually
becomes ventriloquist of his love
of amusing her with his Spanish silence.
She sings in her slow delayed tempo
wearing his tattered bird-costume,
her voice, an offering to the sky,
her body inhabiting the music
of its dark interiority, as the strength
of her tongue pushes beyond language
and hunger. All night she glides
like a swallow over a mirror of water.
He watches her, his ranchera, in his sleep.

'Travailler toujours'

As you trace my reclining figure
and the blades of my shoulders rise
and you use the sight of your hands
to find out what shape I'll take,
closing your eyes and urging me
not to move so you might
lose yourself enough to turn me
into something unbearably real,
the fine line of your hair
abstracts me from the constraints
of form as new images flourish
from the body, new forms
of love pleasing itself
in rooms that won't keep still.

Peonies

In the room where evening comes on
and language loosens on the tip
of the tongue we tap into the sound
of its roots seeking the dark
and the song of the dark
with nothing to hold to but the flower
of the soul with its soul together
when you say something I don't hear
looking for it in the brief pause
your words like water on petals
in the dark of the space that bends
back to what you were saying
the azure eye of it forever blossoming
in the low voice that love talks in.

Found Poem

As for how I got here, it was full of wrong turns
and the corrective contours of snow storms.
Better to try your luck at being lost,
gauging the path by the sound of scythes
and mattocks against invisible heights.
Then, no more shadows, not above nor below
nor beside you; no road at all, no precipice,
gorge or sky: just whiteness out of a dream
from which you can't look away.
I lower my head — a prayer against the bite
of the wind and its swellings. Snow up to my ribs —
labour of breath! At night in the hospice,
you can hear the hosts exhaling noisy canticles
in praise of another day of thieving.

The Abyss

So: you would like to be the swallow
that comes to my window, watching me
talking around the edge of what I mean.
That would explain why you keep glancing
to your left, why the hair on your arms is alert
to the shape on the other side of the glass.
The bird, of course, is your soul.
Why else come back to sit between
these two lamps, looking at my hands
which are busy conducting songs
from the limitations of speech
having crossed the abyss honourably?
It is better not to interrupt the Muse;
it seems she wanted me to love you.

Fairytale

Who are you rising with this morning
in a parallel world to mine not so
far from here? I'm lost in your castle,
as you well know. By what variation
the many ropes of sunlight insist
I hold onto something to attach
this desire to? What variation
on the name of Josette Day — and yet
she is beastly and will forget you
as soon as she leaves. Don't be afraid,
Bête, to look for me in your mirror,
Jeanne de la nuit, whispering to you
in your sleep, from all the mouths
of the statues, your other names.

Coda: Lost Poem

From the other side of the river
softening into that hour
when the scent is released like wine
left to breathe on a mirrored tabletop
it looks as though I have the right idea,
sitting on the boat reading a book,
but it's not so. I keep on with the task
of rewriting the lost poem that turned
mirrors into water and moonlight
into mirrors and water into all manner
and forms of forgetfulness.
The book is merely a cover. Inside it,
the slow work of love, errata of desire,
something written over what is written there.

Notes & Acknowledgements

The poems in *Void Studies* arose from the preoccupation with a detail concerning Arthur Rimbaud who, in about 1872, had considered writing a collection entitled *Études néantes*, consisting of poems which would be written in the spirit of musical études and would go beyond the temptation to convey any direct message.

1. *Études sur Les Illuminations de Rimbaud*, Sergio Sacchi (p.36) – on the poems of spring 1872:

Pierre Brunel a essayé de saisir la tonalité générale de ces pages, en les rattachant à un titre effectivement conçu par Rimbaud: Études néantes. *Certes, aucune preuve objective ne vient étayer ce rapprochement: un tel titre pourrait couvrir aussi un quelconque projet resté à l'état d'ébauche; il n'empêche que le motif, qu'avec Pierre Brunel nous pourrions définir comme « néant », est profondément lié à la saison de l' « alchimie du verbe »; on dirait que la parole elle-même est alors intimement menacée par le silence.*

Pierre Brunel has tried to grasp the general tonality of these pages, by assigning them to the title thought up by Rimbaud: *Études néantes.* No objective evidence can support this association: such a title could be used for any unfinished project; however, the concept of 'néant' we define with Pierre Brunel is deeply linked to the 'alchimie du verbe' season; one could say that the speech itself is intimately menaced by silence.

2. Rimbaud, Projets et réalisations, Pierre Brunel (p.123)
   – quote from Paul Verlaine:

'Sur le tard, je veux dire vers dix-sept ans au plus tard, Rimbaud s'avisa d'assonances, de rythmes qu'il appelait « néants » et il avait même l'idée d'un recueil: Etudes néantes, *qu'il n'écrivit à ma connaissance pas.'*

'Later, I would say when he was about seventeen or so, Rimbaud utilized assonances, rhythms, calling them *"néants"* and he even thought about a collection *Etudes néantes*, which he never wrote as far I know.'

3. *Introduction à l'ordinaire*, Serge Durno (p.60):

Si nous ne comprenons pas la dite de Rimbaud, ce n'est pas toujours parce qu'il se laisse aller à des associations d'idées quasi auto-matiques ou parce qu'il décrit ses rêves. Verlaine nous a révélé que Rimbaud avait le projet d'études néantes. Il se pourrait bien que Les Illuminations *soient le résultat de ces études ou ces études elles-mêmes.*

If we don't understand the writing of Rimbaud, it's not always because he plays with quasi-automatic associations of ideas or because he describes dreams. Verlaine has revealed that Rimbaud had a project called *Études néantes*. It's possible that *Les Illu-minations* could be the result of these studies or be the studies themselves.

*

Album

Partly assembled from phrasings in a letter dated 15 November 1885 from Mallarmé to Verlaine, reprinted in *Divagations*, translated by Barbara Johnson (Harvard University Press, 2009).

Found Poem

Largely assembled from phrasings in a letter dated 17 November 1878 from Rimbaud to his family, translated from the French by Wyatt Mason; this appeared in *The Paris Review*, 17 November 2015.

*

Thanks are due to the editors of the following magazines and publications in which some of these poems, or versions of them, first appeared: *The Compass Magazine, The Dark Horse, The Edinburgh Review, Ploughshares, Poetry London, The Scores.*

Many thanks to the Royal Literary Fund for financial support.

Special thanks are due to Jerome Andre, Ciaran Carson and Don Paterson for their invaluable contributions during the preparation of this book.